Australian Defence Force Machines

Aaron White

www.facebook.com/childrensbooksbyaaronwhite
www.childrensbooksbyaaronwhite.com

DEDICATION

I dedicate this book to my beautiful wife, Francesca, and to my wonderful sons, Tyler and Jayden. I also dedicate it to all of the Fantastic Defence Force personnel. You men and women do such an amazing job, and I hope this book will help to show people what you do. Thank you.

Copyright © 2017 Aaron White
All rights reserved.

ISBN-13: 978-0-9943915-4-4

The Australian Defence Force uses lots of different machines to keep Australia safe.

Come and meet some of these Awesome Machines.

We will start with Jayden, the Jet.

Hello, I am Jayden, the Jet. I can fly very fast, through the sky. If an aircraft is in an area, which it is not allowed to be in, I can fly up to them and ask them to, please, leave.

Howdy, my name is Gemma, the G-Wagon. I am a four-wheel drive vehicle, and I can go up and down steep hills, and through muddy areas, without getting stuck.

It is lots of fun.

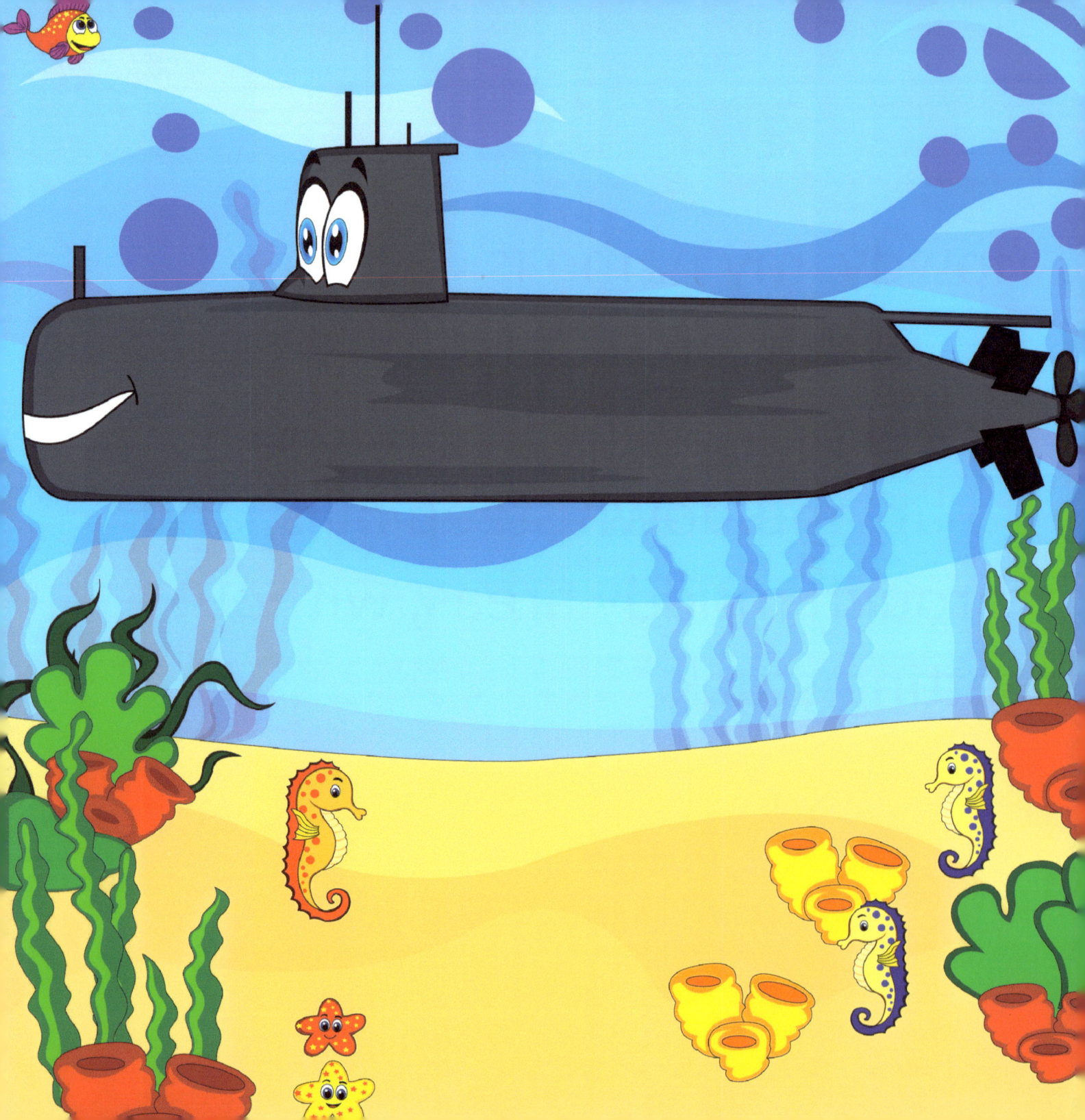

Hi, I am Colin, the Submarine. I can swim under the water, for a very long time.

I like to sneak up to the boats that are on top of the water and surprise them.

G'day, I am Tyler, the Tank. I use my cannon to shoot shells across long distances to hit the enemy tanks. Shells are like big bullets.

I am also covered in lots of metal, called armour. This armour protects me from getting hurt if I am shot.

I am Reece, the Ridge Hull Inflatable Boat. I take my diver friends to places in the ocean and rivers so that they can go for a dive.

It must look so cool underwater, with all those fish and coral.

Hi, I am Betty, the Black Hawk Helicopter. If someone has been injured, I can fly into the area, pick them up, and then take them to a safe location.

I like helping people.

Hello, I am Paul, the Patrol Boat. I travel along the Australian coastline, making sure that no one is trying to get into Australia, who is not allowed to be here.

Hi, my name is Hercules, the Military Transport Aircraft. I am very big and strong. I have four powerful engines on my wings, which help me to fly the soldiers wherever they want to go.

I hope that was fun, meeting all of those Awesome Defence Force Machines.

I have left some blank pages for you to draw your favourite defence force machines on.

www.ingramcontent.com/pod-product-compliance
Lightning Source LLC
Chambersburg PA
CBHW041439010526
44118CB00002B/125